The CHEER UP Do

Taro Gomi

chronicle books · san francisco

When you're feeling sad or lonely, try **doodling**. Soon you'll feel much better!

How does your face look when you're sad?

Let's draw a **shy** moon.

Let's draw a bashful person in this house.

Let's worriedly arrange some flowers.

Let's draw a really dismal meal.

Let's draw someone glumly riding the bike.

What time is it on this confused clock?

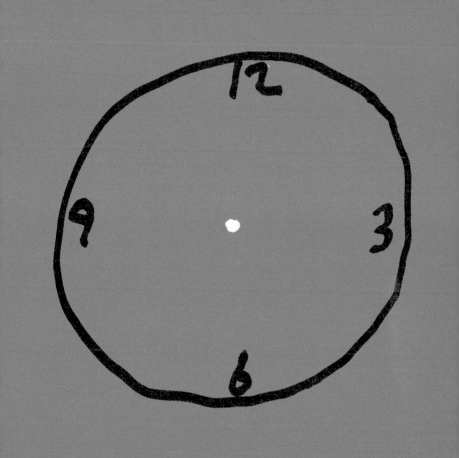

Let's color this horse
with sad colors.

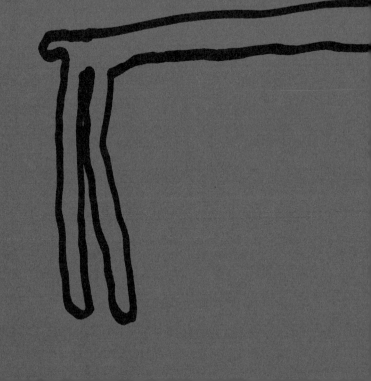

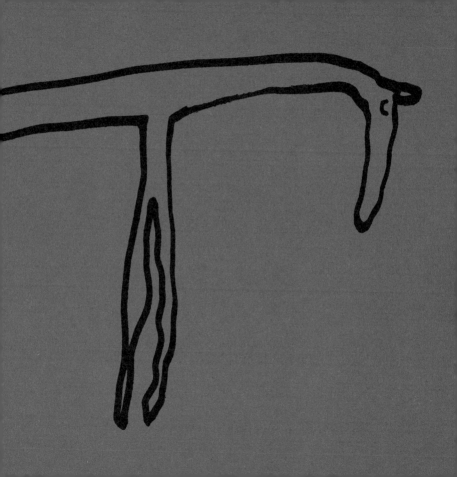

Let's draw a **puzzled** person kicking the ball.

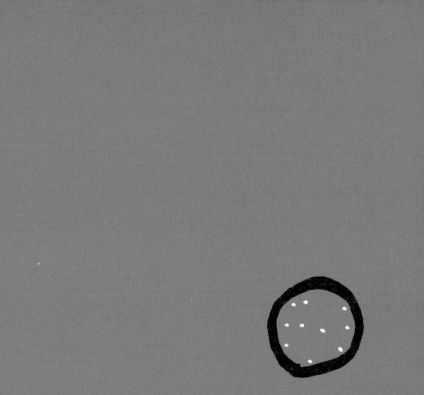

Let's draw a miserable monster.

**Put a discombobulated
little bird on this tree.**

**Let's draw a
flustered person
walking in the rain.**

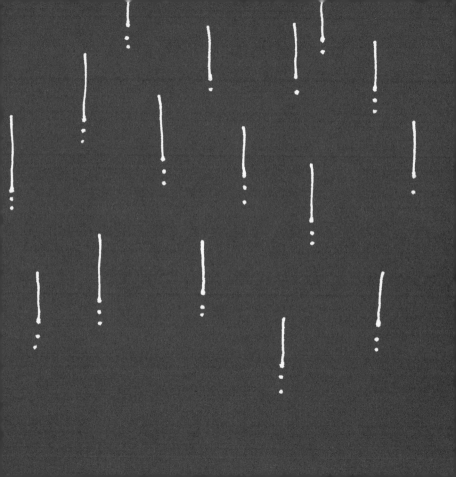

What kind of umbrella does a disappointed person carry?

Let's draw an embarrassed snowman.

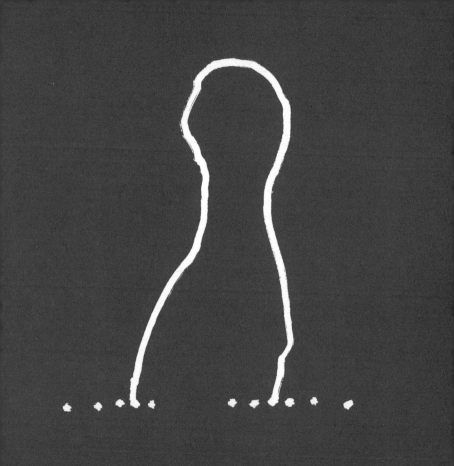

Let's draw a reticent letter **A**.

What kind of clothes do you wear when you're distressed?

Please draw a snake that is even more unhappy than this one.

Can you help this bewildered cat?

**Let's do some math
to feel better.**

$$\begin{array}{r} 18 \\ -\ 5 \\ \hline \end{array}$$

Let's cheer up this forlorn little boat.

The cow is sad to be
all alone. Draw some
friends for her.

What kind of bow does she wear when she's feeling down?

**Please make this
sad clown happy.**

What a lonely little fruit shop. Please add customers to make it busy.

What? You're not sad anymore? What does your face look like now? Yes, you're doing fine. Turn the page to doodle more!

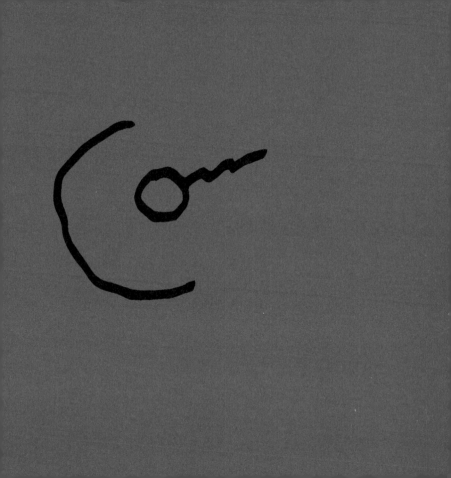

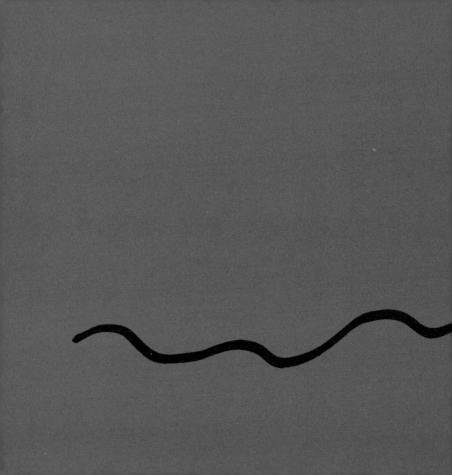

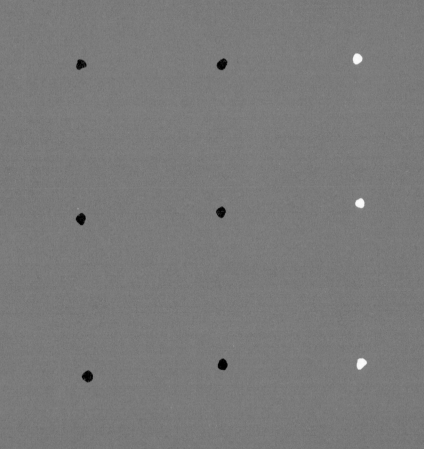

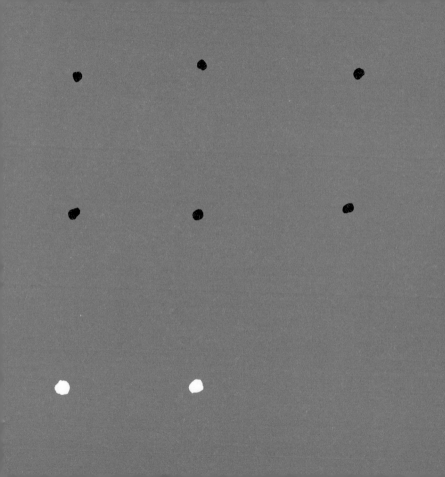

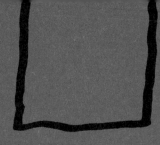

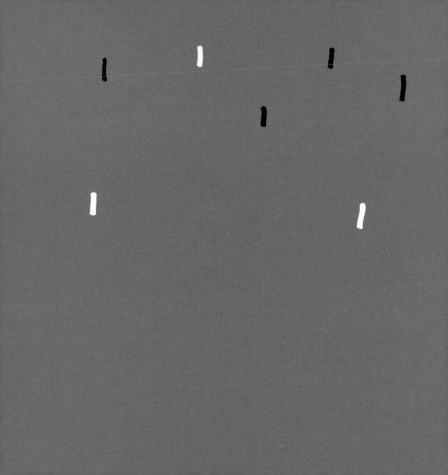

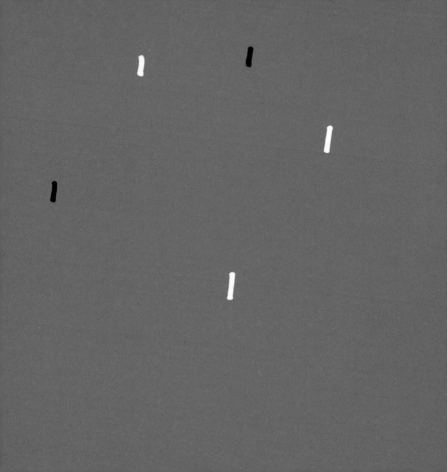

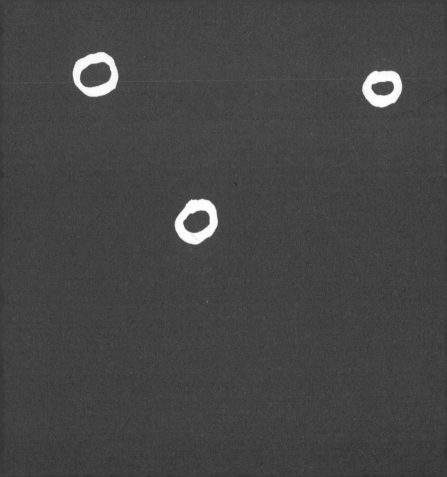

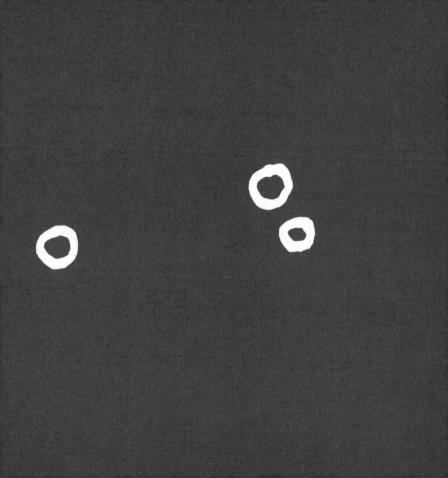

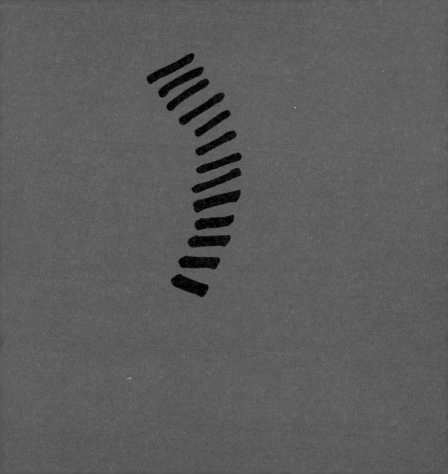

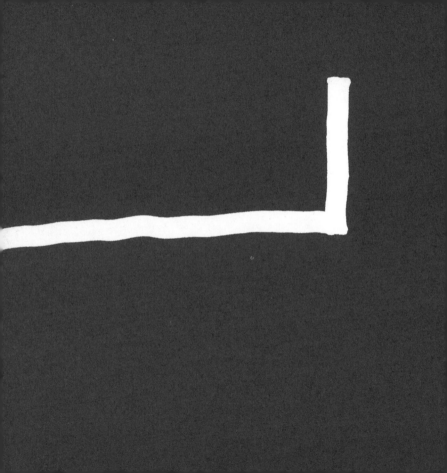

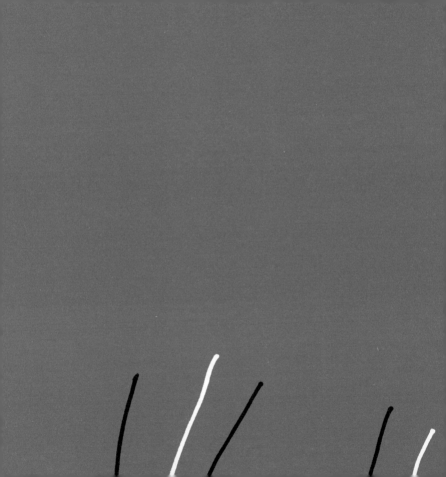

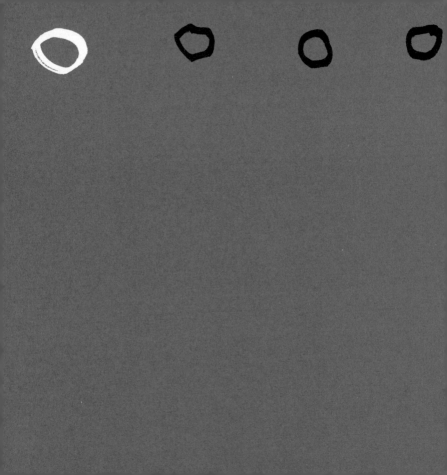

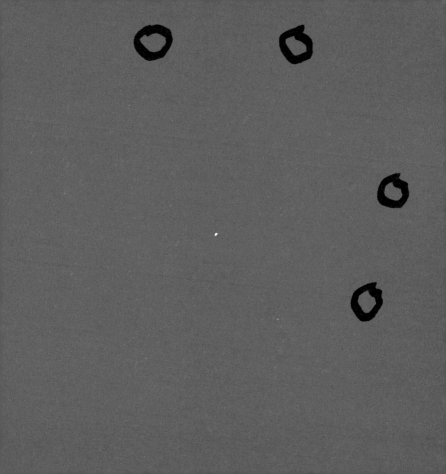

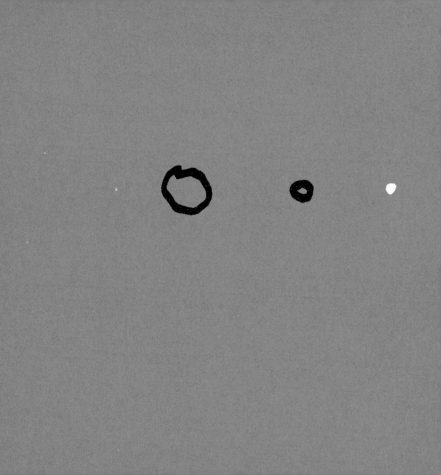

Let's make this a stripy cat.

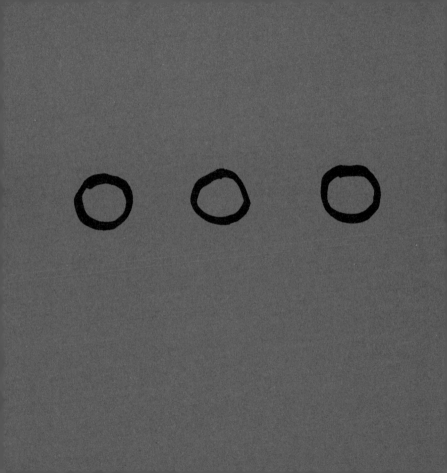

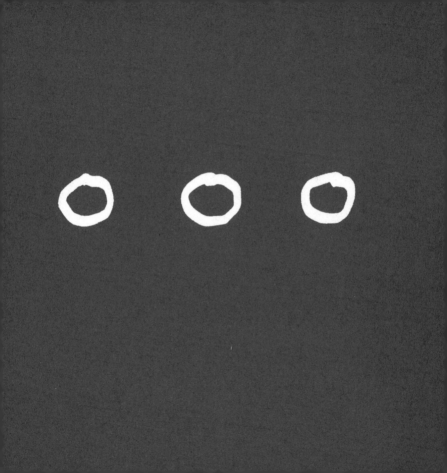

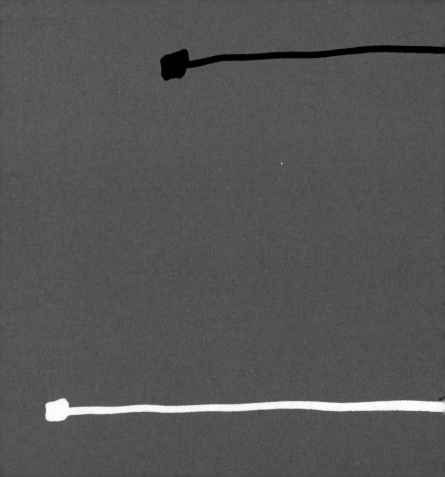

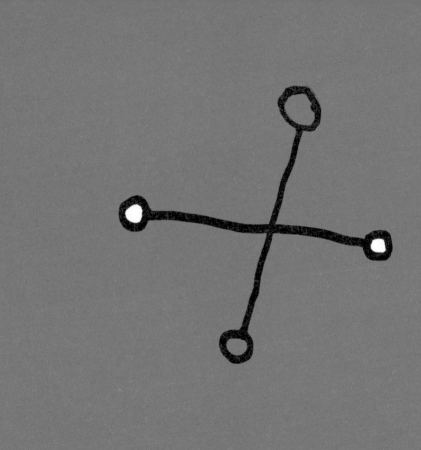

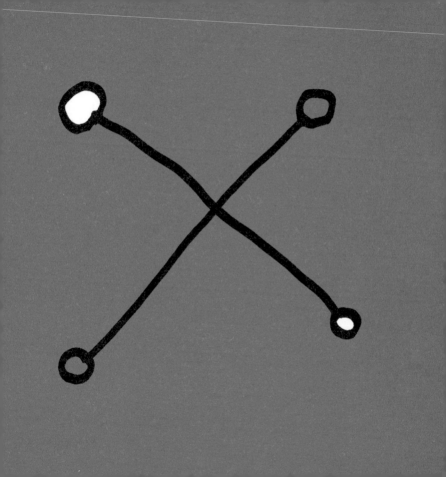

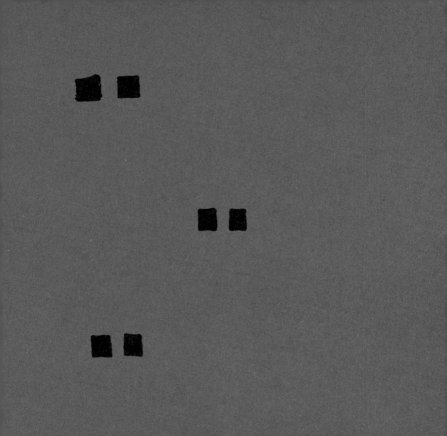

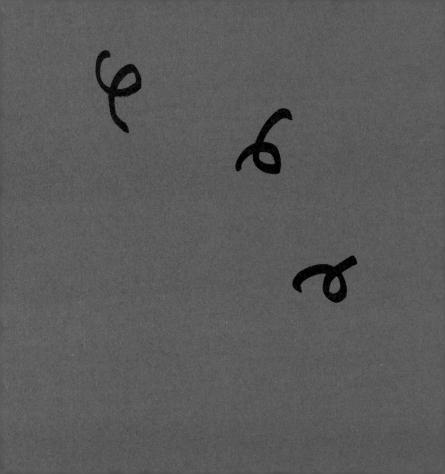

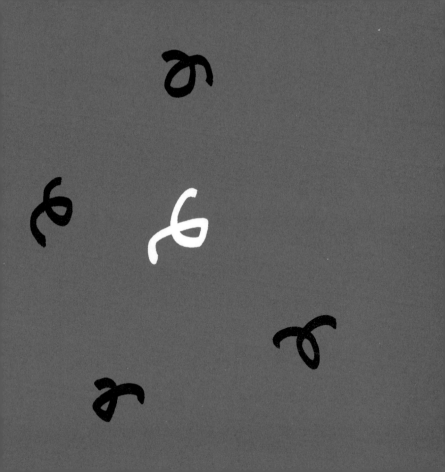

Let's draw a **delicious-looking hamburger!**

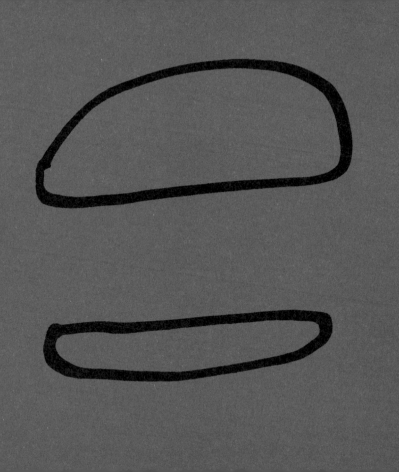

Let's draw a **delicious-looking** sandwich!

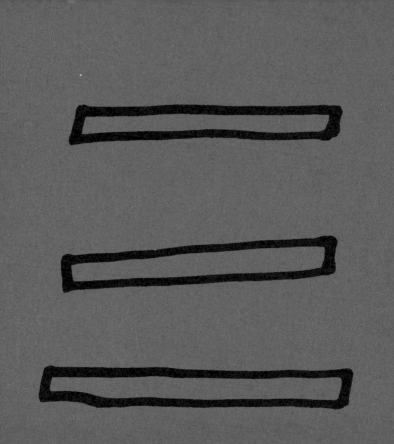

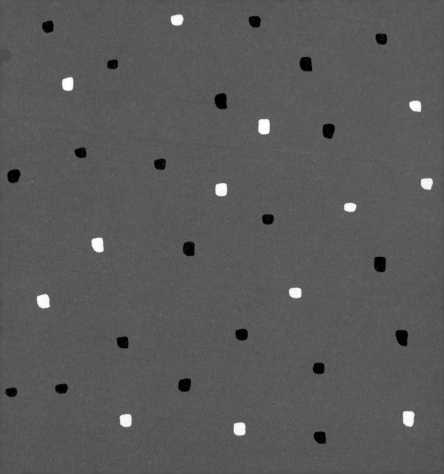

This kid is having a tantrum.

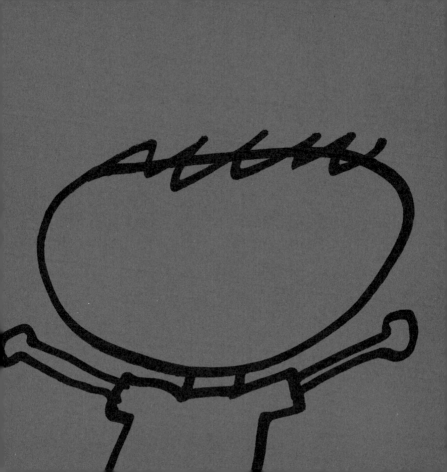

Who is on the swing?

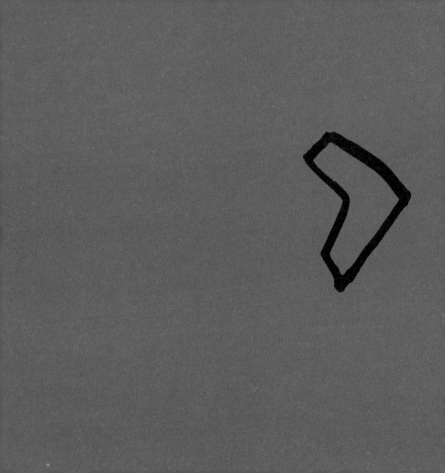

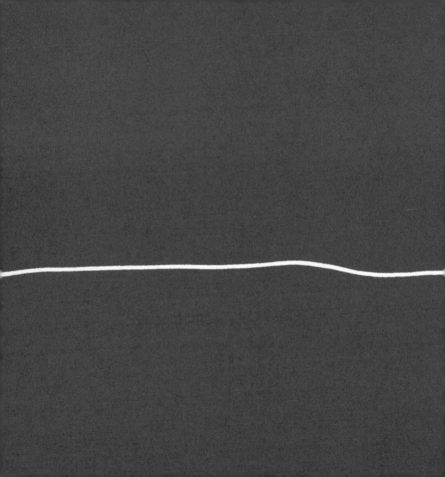

Who is sitting on the bench?

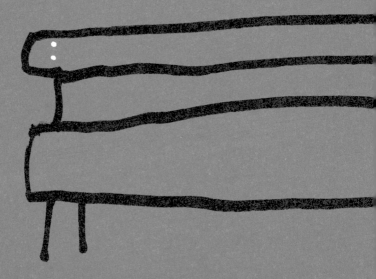

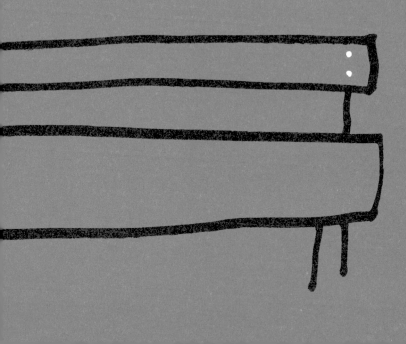

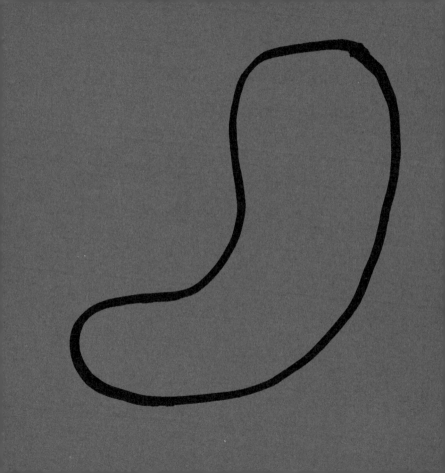

Let's draw a mask!

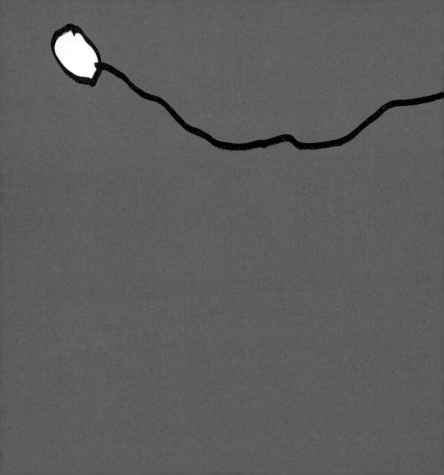

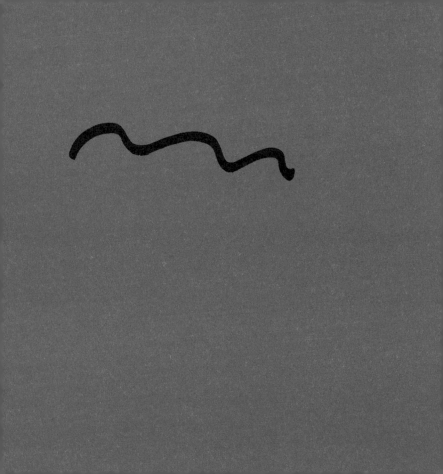

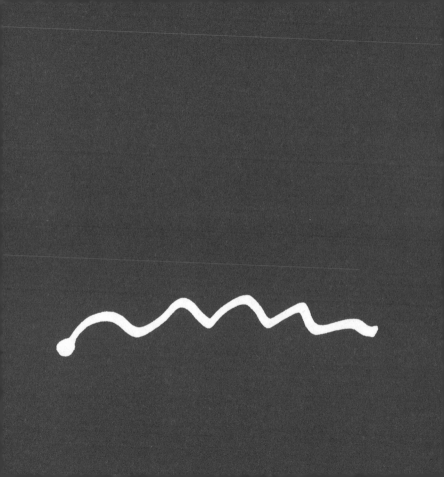

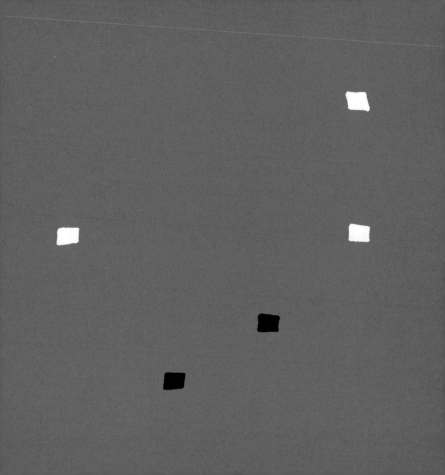

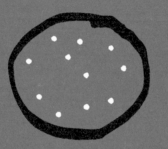

What's in your hand?

What kind of packages are on the truck?

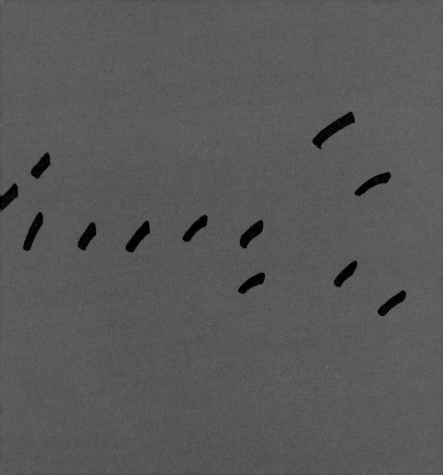

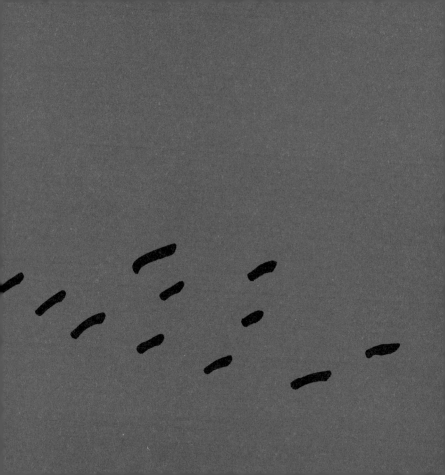

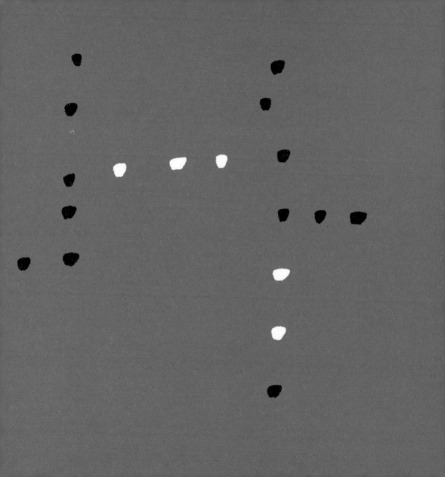

Who is underground?

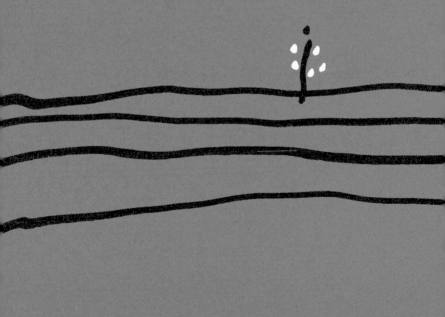

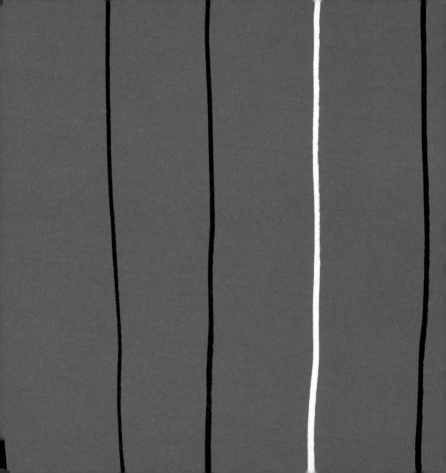

What time is it?

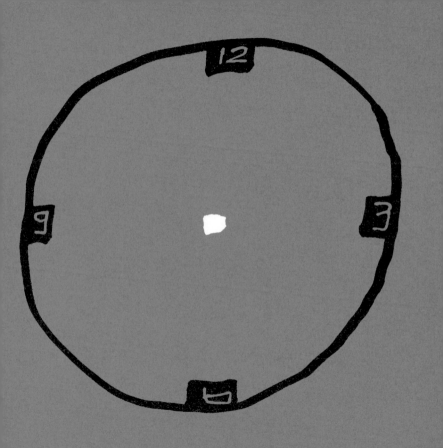

Please draw a mane, a tail, and anything else the horse needs.

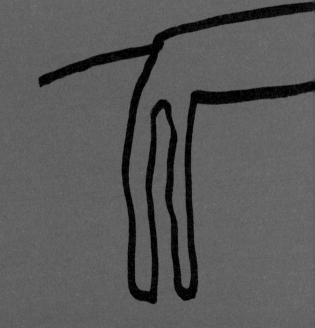

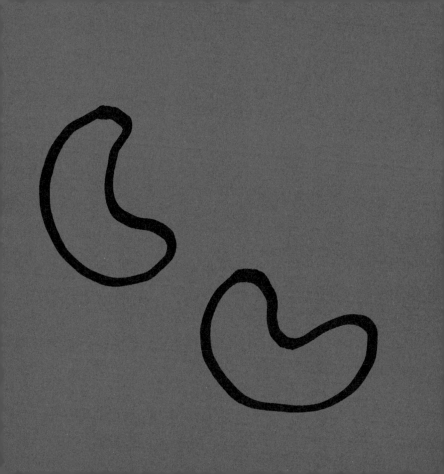

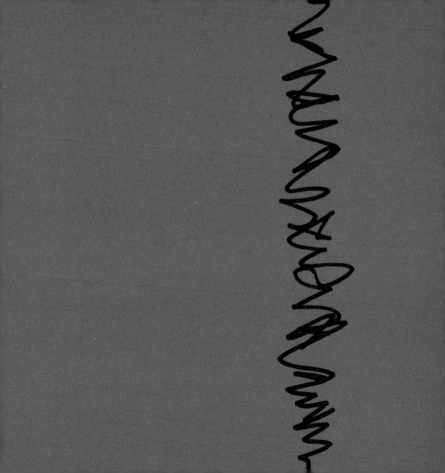

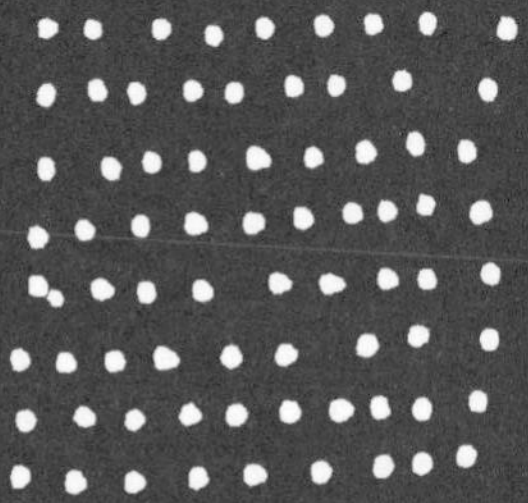

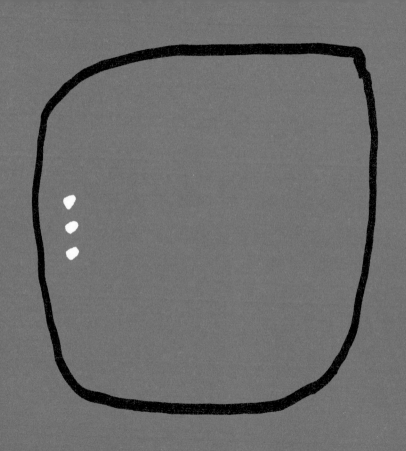

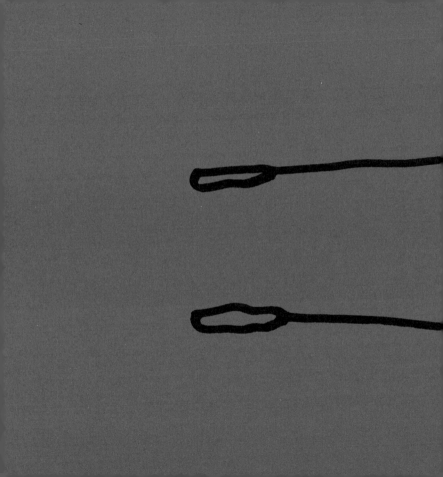

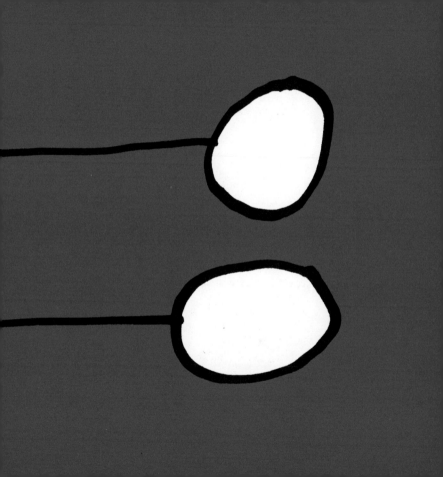

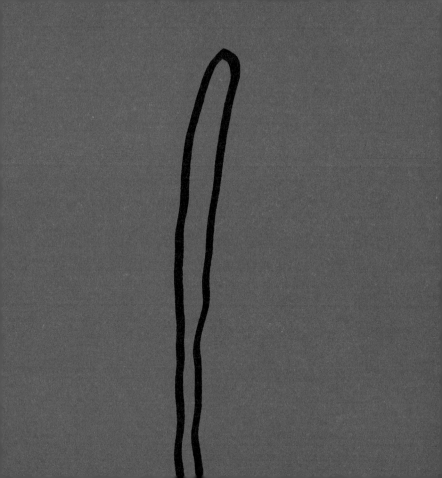

Someone is walking up the hill.

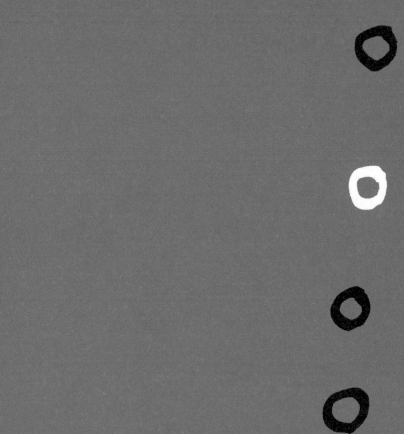

What kind of hairstyle will you give this kid?

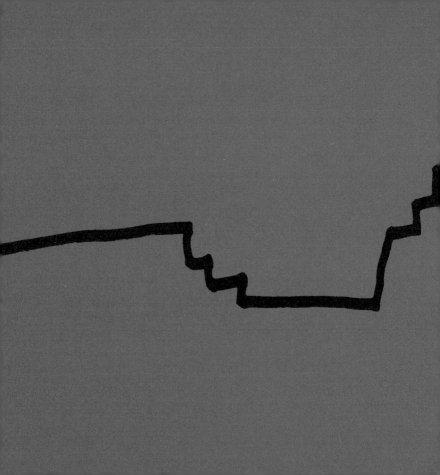

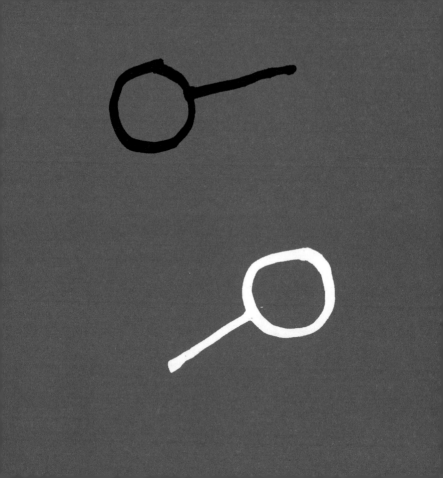

Let's draw some windows.

Whose house is this?

Who is in the hot air balloon?

Which one is crying?
Which one is smiling?

Let's all eat the feast!

Doodling
is always
lots of
fun. Let's
doodle
again!

Original edition published in Japan by BRONZE PUBLISHING Inc., Tokyo,
under the title *Kanashii Tokino Rakugaki Book*. Copyright © 2010 Taro Gomi.

First United States edition published in 2012 by Chronicle Books LLC.
English text copyright © 2012 by Chronicle Books LLC.
All rights reserved.

ISBN 978-1-4521-0776-9

Manufactured in Singapore.
Typeset in Avenir.

1 3 5 7 9 10 8 6 4 2

Chronicle Books LLC
680 Second Street, San Francisco, California 94107
www.chroniclekids.com